# Contents

D0097344

# When a Loved One Dies

*Meditations*

*for the*

*Journey*

*through*

*Grief*

*Philip W. Williams*

Augsburg
MINNEAPOLIS

*To Nancy, Jason, Jenna,*
*who are life for me.*

Cover design by David Meyer
Book design by Michelle L. Norstad

ISBN 0-8066-4269-6 (alk. paper)

The paper used in this publication meets the minimum requirements of American National Standard for Information Sciences—Permanence of Paper for Printed Library Materials, ANSI Z329.48-1984. ♾ ™

Manufactured in the U.S.A.                                                                                          AF 9-4269

05      04      03      02      01      1      2      3      4      5      6      7      8      9      10

# Preface

*"Blessed are those who mourn,* for they will be comforted" (Matthew 5:4). This is good news to any of us who has been deprived, robbed of a life, who has lost a loved one. Jesus, our Lord, with intuitive sensitivity toward people, encouraged grief and bereavement. He was saying: "Do it! Grieve!" Why? He knew its potential for good. He knew we would eventually receive blessing and comfort. Jesus saw no virtue in being tough-as-nails, brave, unfeeling, stoical when experiencing the loss of a loved one. Experiencing the loss, having and showing feelings, reexamining attitudes and beliefs—all are necessary and Christian. To grieve and go through bereavement is to move from hurt to health. If we do not go through bereavement, bitterness, sickness, and even death may result.

Jesus knew that grief and bereavement were normal and necessary. He also knew that when we give ourselves permission to do this work—and it *is* work—we will receive God's blessing. We will be able to affirm life once again.

There is no "typical grieving person." Each of us is only typical of what is particular and peculiar to herself or himself. There are many common grief reactions, but we each experience the loss of a loved one in our own way.

This book is not meant to be a book of what you, as a grieving person, "should" be experiencing. This book doesn't describe the "right and only way" to grieve successfully. Many sections will ring true for you: "That's how I feel. That's me. That's where I am." Some sections will seem unrelated, inapplicable, perhaps farfetched. Other sections may hit too close and be rejected.

But you are you, and this is your book. Make this book yours in whatever way it applies to you. You don't need to start at the beginning. Read whatever section seems to strike your present need, feeling, or curiosity.

God bless you in your bereavement journey—not a journey without pain, but an adventurous journey that can be, in time, graciously good.

# It Can't Be True

*A mother and father walked down the hospital corridor* from the emergency room to a waiting room, filled with fearful anticipation. Wrinkles of tense pain showed on their faces. All they could hear was the sound of their own shoes on the marble hallway.

In the waiting room the dreaded news came, straight and simple. "We did all we could to save her. I'm sorry, but your daughter has died."

The mother began to shake. Screams, tears, agony poured out. "No, no, it can't be true. Not my little girl!" The father sat silently, rigid. Slowly tears came, forcing their way out of eyes that had just seen a truth he couldn't believe. Shock set in. "It just can't be true."

News of the death of a loved one may create within us a temporary numbness or state of anesthesia. This is an eerie unreal feeling, but it is natural, necessary, and helpful. Shock is a built-in buffer that helps us tolerate the overwhelming news or fearful scenes of death.

God has built into us this natural buffer for the initial blow. It is a good gift because it protects us. There is no way for any of us to totally comprehend the initial loss of a loved person. Shock numbs us and gives us time to get ready for our bereavement journey. We need it, yet only for a time. Then we must move on. Yet, as we move into our bereavement journey, it is common to revert back to the time of shock. One husband said, "My wife died two years ago, but I still have moments when it seems that she really hasn't died." These flashes occur, but they don't stay.

God has given us a good gift in shock. It is a clue that we are in the beginning of our journey. We may feel we can't go on, or that we never will want to go on, but it is good to know that we have been protected in the midst of an overwhelming, painful loss.

### ✆ Scripture Meditation: Psalm 77:1-2, 11-12

I cry aloud to God,
aloud to God, that he may hear me.
In the day of my trouble I seek the Lord;
in the night my hand is stretched out without wearying;
my soul refuses to be comforted.
I will call to mind the deeds of the Lord;
I will remember your wonders of old.
I will meditate on all your work,
and muse on your mighty deeds.

*Dear Father, I hurt, and I need protection. Help me to understand that shock is a sign of your built-in protection to help me weather the fury of the storm. As the storm slowly fades, help me to leave the shock and to move forward in my bereavement and in my life. Amen.*

# I Don't Believe It

*After the headlines, comics, letters to the editor, and sports,* many people turn to the obituary column. The language used in an obituary announcement is revealing: "Mr. Edward Praif passed away December 3." "Mrs. Lucille Agner was promoted to glory last evening." "Wanda Sue Smith was taken Wednesday evening." We know death is real, yet our language often reveals our difficulty in accepting the reality of death. "Death" and "die" are practically obscene words to some people. It's as if saying those words will make the death of a loved one too real.

Denial is natural. If we see something that offends our sight, we close our eyes. If something stinks, we hold our nose. If something is ugly, we try to make it look pretty and pleasing. When we lose a loved one through death, we may normally and naturally deny our deep loss for a time. Yet, if this denial continues and we suppress the reality of this death, we may become ill and need help.

I have often heard people remark how "well" someone took their loved one's death. The bereaved appeared controlled, having everything in hand, perhaps managing to be a superb host or hostess during the early bereavement process. This may be, but it can also hold back the inner struggle to admit the reality of death, "I don't believe it" or "I *won't* believe it."

But we need not be "cool heroes" when a loved one dies. We are human beings created by a God who knows the heart of life and of humans. We are created by a God who knows that denial can fortify hope and prevent despair—for a time. But prolonged, total denial can only lead to a despair that sees no hope, no triumph.

Recall the number of times Jesus attempted to prepare his disciples for his death. They wouldn't hear of it. They denied it. Few people want to hear the words of impending death, yet Jesus urged them to be prepared and to move through denial to acceptance and hope.

I still recall the words of a twelve-year-old daughter to her parents, who had steadfastly denied her impending death: "Don't worry, I'm going to die today, but it's OK. I'm going to be with Jesus." These words showed her own acceptance, and they could have helped her parents move from "I won't believe it" to "I do believe it."

### ∞ Scripture Meditation: John 11:21-26

Martha said to Jesus, "Lord, if you had been here, my brother would not have died. But even now I know that God will give you whatever you ask of him." Jesus said to her, "Your brother will rise again."

Martha said to him, "I know that he will rise again in the resurrection on the last day." Jesus said to her, "I am the resurrection and the life. Those who believe in me, even though they die, will live, and everyone who lives and believes in me will never die."

*Dear God, I find it hard to accept things I don't want to be true. How can I bear up in the face of my loss? If I face my loss, I might lose control. I might have to feel pain rather than feeling nothing. Help me not to fight so hard to deny the death of my loved one. Help me to move in my journey with you. I trust you. I know you will not leave me. Amen.*

# If Only

*Do you think if we had left sooner for the hospital* it would have made a difference?"

"She never would tell us when she had those pains, but I could tell. If only I had insisted and dragged her to the doctor."

"I shouldn't have let him go out tonight. I had a feeling . . ."

"What if we had gone to the Medical Center instead of here? They have more specialists. Maybe they could have done something."

There is always some guilt when any of us loses a loved one. This isn't unusual. None of us can live close to another person and love deeply without hurting that person. We do and say things we later regret. We know they hurt our loved one.

Intimacy and closeness are built by loving and hurting and reconciling. We can't really learn to love unless we are willing to run the risks of hurting and failing. Losing someone we love reminds us of those hurts and failings, of words we regret saying, incidents we'd like to forget, actions we'd like to take back. We feel guilty.

Or we may be that person who has stayed faithfully in the waiting room of an intensive care unit hour after hour, day after day. Then we leave the ill person as fatigue, home responsibilities, and family needs set in, or as the loved one seems to regain strength. What happens if this loved person suddenly takes a turn for the worse and dies? We blame ourselves for not having been there.

If we were to continue in this "if only" guilt, we would be unrealistically assuming that our presence would have made the difference in our loved one's living or dying. We would be assuming an unreal power and control over life and death; a power and control we simply do not possess. An analyst said to Robert Anderson, "You are experiencing a guilt that denies what we are, which is, of course, a human being—fallible, needful, of limited saintliness."

It hurts deeply not to have been there when our loved one died. We feel guilt because we wanted to be there. But if this guilt is prolonged, we may need some professional help in working through it.

When we feel we are beginning to accept ourselves, guilt's hold is broken. One grieving person said, "I began to realize there was no more I could do. As I let go of my guilt, I felt more at ease with myself. I began to like myself. I experienced the assurance of forgiveness which the pastor pronounces each week in the worship service."

God has provided some beautiful resources to help us in our guilt. Church worship contains public or private confession and absolution. The Scriptures proclaim an accepting Lord who continually forgives people. This same Lord and Savior died for us in an ultimate act of forgiveness, and he rose to give us new life. He has given us the Lord's Supper to strengthen us and to reconcile us with God.

Guilt is real. The Bible shows us our guilt, but it also reveals a gracious God who forgives us. A college professor once said something that speaks to many life crises, certainly to the guilt of "if only." He said, "The greatest prayer anyone can pray is, 'Create in me a clean heart, O God, and renew a right spirit within me.'"

### ∼ Scripture Meditation: Psalm 25:6-7

Be mindful of your mercy, O Lord, and of your steadfast love,
for they have been from of old.
Do not remember the sins of my youth or my transgressions;
according to your steadfast love remember me,
for your goodness' sake, O Lord!

*Dear God, I get so entangled with my doubts, my regrets, my wrongs. I even plague myself with my guilt. Get through to me, Lord! I need to know that there is forgiveness and acceptance with you. I need to accept myself. Remind me of the cross, the greatest sign of your forgiveness. Amen.*

# I Could Cry

*Mrs. Brown had lost her husband* after a sudden heart attack.

"You look like you could cry."

"I won't."

"Why not?"

"I prefer to do it when I'm alone. When I get started I can't stop. I'll let it out when I'm finally home." But she didn't cry, even at home.

A man had just seen his ten-year-old daughter die. He choked back tears. Relatives encouraged him to hold on, to be brave: "Don't cry!" Rather than expressing the hurt of his loss, he pleased the uptight relatives as long as he could.

The friends and relatives said, "Weren't they remarkably strong and poised? They really went through the funeral well. You have to admire them." But do we?

What is wrong with tears? The idea that big boys or big girls don't cry is a mistaken assumption. Not to cry, ever, is unnatural and borders on being inhuman.

Many of us have been led to believe that crying is not good. In men it is thought unmanly, a sign of weakness. But we forget that when he lost his good friend Lazarus, "Jesus wept." We may have learned this as the shortest verse in the Bible. We may not have learned its basic human message: "Cry! It's good. It's human. It's Christian."

Nine-year-old Tommy had lost his grandfather. During the funeral vigil, Tommy and an old friend, Mr. Walters, talked together. Tommy asked, "Mr. Walters, do you ever cry?"

The old man answered, "Yes I do. I cried when your grandfather died, for grandpa was my friend, too."

Tommy said, "I didn't cry! Why did you cry?"

"I cry when I'm hurt," Mr. Walters replied. "I was deeply hurt by grandpa's death. It was a hard loss. He was such a good friend to me and even more to you."

Eventually Tommy cried, too.

Tears don't erase all the hurt. Tears don't bring the dead to life. But tears do help to ease the pain.

In their book on grief, Bernadine Kries and Alice Pattie tell about a young widow who was told by everyone not to cry in front of her six-year-old daughter. They said it would leave emotional scars. She took their advice, and it proved to be bad. One day her daughter asked, "Why didn't you love daddy? You were glad he died!"

This young widow then realized what she had done by not crying in front of her daughter. They then cried together, and things were easier for both of them.

When Jesus drew near to Jerusalem shortly before his own death, he saw the city, and he wept over it. Jesus cried over a city and its people! How much more we need to show our hurt when death claims a loved one.

### ∽ Scripture Meditation: 2 Corinthians 1:3-4

Blessed be the God and Father of our Lord Jesus Christ, the Father of mercies and the God of all consolation, who consoles us in all our affliction, so that we may be able to console those who are in any affliction with the consolation with which we ourselves are consoled by God.

*Dear God, Jesus points the way for me to be honest with my feelings. Sometimes I fear embarrassment or misunderstanding. Sometimes I fear being pitied or put down. Sometimes I fear the intensity of my own hurt. Help me to understand and express what I feel. If you understand, I can, too. Amen.*

# I'm Mad

*What happens when a person I love dies?* Dare I be angry? Is it wrong for a Christian to be angry?

When friends lost a child in an automobile accident, I was angry and questioned, "God, why? Why?" Job's wife was even more direct. When her children died, she angrily shouted at Job, "Curse God and die!"

We are God's people, humans with feelings. This includes a capacity for experiencing the emotion of anger. If we lose a person or thing close to us, we react. Any relationship of worth is filled with rich, personal investment. We don't want to lose this. When we do, we very well can feel anger. We may feel it like an erupting inner volcano or it may be a "slow burn." We may feel a general irritability or a lingering bitterness. Some bereaved people have used words such as the following to describe anger: "I could flare up at anytime"; "Stupid little things upset me"; "My nerves are on edge"; "I feel a turmoil inside."

To feel angry is natural, normal. To be angry is a potential part of the healing process. This is a part of being a bereaved Christian. To suppress anger and never let it out can lead to a deeper than normal depression.

We may be angry at God. It is hard to accept that life is unsure and that death is an uncertain certainty. These thoughts make us feel powerless. Being angry is a natural, desperate attempt by us to control the order of things, because God seems to have let us down.

The anger may be at people around us. I vividly recall the death of my favorite dog, Brownie, when I was a young boy. He was hit by a jeep and left at the road's edge. Walking beside my father, I pulled the little wagon that carried my friend. I felt anger well up. I lashed out at the neighbors who drove that jeep and killed my friend. To me, that wasn't a dog, that was a person! If a dog is a person to a child, what about a loved one who really is a person?

The anger may be at those who cared for our loved ones—doctors, nurses, other medical personnel, relatives. It certainly may be directed at people who press us toward accepting our loss too soon, before we've worked through our feelings and thoughts.

We may even be angry at our loved one. As one lady very honestly admitted, "I'm so angry at Joe for dying first! He always took care of the finances. I never did any of that. Now I have to, and I'm at a loss. It's too much!" This may seem cruel and disrespectful. It is no doubt self-pitying. But, it is also an intense expression of anger that comes when a person is left alone, feeling helpless and insecure. It isn't abnormal or sinful.

We may be angry at ourselves, berating ourselves for what we said and did, or didn't say and didn't do. There is no way to say and do all we may ideally wish, for we are not God. Even knowing this does not mean we don't feel angry.

St. Paul encouraged the Ephesians to let their anger out, not to hold it in. "Be angry, but do not sin; do not let the sun go down on your anger, and give no opportunity to the devil." Isn't it conceivable that if we really do believe that God is Father, he will be the best of fathers? This kind of parent knows us and allows us the expression of fullest feelings, including our anger. As a loving, understanding parent, we are accepted in our anger without reservation.

### Scripture Meditation: Psalm 22:28-29

For dominion belongs to the Lord,
and he rules over the nations.
To him, indeed, shall all who sleep in the earth bow down;
before him shall bow all who go down to the dust,
and I shall live for him.

*Why do I want to lash out at you, Lord? I feel guilty blaming you, but I feel so hurt, so angry. I know somehow that you will understand even when I don't understand. You are my Father. Amen.*

# Depressed

*"My God, My God, why have you forsaken me?* Why are you so far from helping me, from the words of my groaning? O my God, I cry by day, but you do not answer; and by night, but find no rest" (Psalm 22:1-2).

"How long, O LORD? Will you forget me forever? How long will you hide your face from me?" (Psalm 13:1).

The Psalms sound out the all-too-familiar cry or whimper of depression. Shakespeare put it another way when he said, "The grief that does not speak/whispers the o'erfraught heart and bids it break."

The drawn face of Steve, who stood statue-like in his work clothes, gave way to matching words: "I'm feeling so low. I don't care. I can't get going. What's the use anyway? No one cares or knows what I feel. There's no God of love."

Depression! It's a sudden or gradual "going down," a lowering of emotion that goes much lower than on a usual bad day. With it comes a companion, isolation. Mrs. Young said it well: "I want to get away. I don't care about anybody. I wish people would just leave me alone." This is a scary feeling for many of us. We don't like to feel down, even though the death of our loved one gives us reason to feel that way. Depression is unpleasant. It has the odor of hopelessness hanging around it. Every cloud does not have a silver lining. In fact, when we're depressed, no cloud has a silver lining.

To have someone say, "You'll just have to get over it. Cheer up a little. Don't worry, you'll be OK," seems cruel. We may want to say something in angry retaliation, but we silently force a strained smile, at best. Behind this is the feeling, "Get away, you don't know. It won't pass!"

When we lose someone close to us, we can expect depression. There is no way to avoid feeling "down and out" when death takes someone we love. We certainly can't be happy and cheerful! Depression comes like a known but unwelcomed companion to stay for a while. When it does, the dark clouds blot out the sun. Sleep may be difficult. Food doesn't seem important. We may sob quietly. Our memory may seem shifted into neutral. Some fears about "what may happen" creep in. Depression invades everything we are and do. It may completely immobilize us. When it does, especially when this immobilization is prolonged, we need professional help.

Facing the fullness of death is depressing. Naomi told me that when she realized the impact of death, she felt as if she had fallen into a dark pit. She felt separated from everyone and everything. Nothing mattered. She couldn't pray. Her faith seemed to disappear. As time passed and she attempted to relate to her friends and relatives, to become more active, often at the gentle "push and shove" of people who really cared for her, she began to feel the clouds of depression slowly move away. As they moved, her faith emerged, as if it had been there, but obscured. She could pray. She could continue her mourning and face her loss. Depression was a sign that she was really facing her loved one's death. It was a signpost to recovery when she began to move through it. Naomi was experiencing not only Jesus' forsakenness on the cross, but also his resurrection power, as she came alive within herself and in her relationship to others.

### ∽ Scripture Meditation: Romans 8:26-27

Likewise the Spirit helps us in our weakness; for we do not know how to pray as we ought, but that very Spirit intercedes with sighs too deep for words. And God, who searches the heart, knows what is the mind of the Spirit, because the Spirit intercedes for the saints according to the will of God.

*Dear God and Father, I feel hopeless and helpless. I feel all light has gone out. Even if I don't reach out to others, let me allow them to reach in to me. I long to experience again that you have not forsaken me. You are faithful and true. Help me to be faithful, too. Through Jesus Christ, my risen Lord. Amen.*

# I'm Not
# Feeling Well

*The psalmist said that we are "fearfully and wonderfully made."* There is little, if anything, we experience that doesn't affect our total person. When I'm physically exhausted, I have a hard time thinking clearly and quickly. When I'm upset about a relationship, my feelings churn and, as a result, my stomach may ache or my muscles cramp. Our mourning the death of a loved one affects us totally, too.

Mr. Martin sat slumped across from me and said, "Ever since she's gone it hasn't been the same."

"What do you mean?" I asked.

"Well, she was for one thing a real good cook. Couldn't beat her. Made everything from scratch. Not many women do that nowadays. Yes sir! I guess I got pretty much used to her cooking. I suppose she spoiled me. I just haven't eaten right since she's gone. In fact, I haven't had much appetite for anything."

It's not unusual for our grief to give us physical distress. The loss of appetite, loss of weight, and loss of energy, are quite normal. Some of us may react differently, perhaps starting to eat too much. In either case, our bodies feel our personal loss keenly.

One middle-aged widow started having headaches though she never had them before. Her rheumatism started acting up again. She couldn't understand this until she realized that these physical problems had started shortly after her husband's death. She began to see the connection. Her loss was hard to face, and her body was trying to force her to do it. As she talked, releasing her feelings, the physical symptoms of her grief lessened. She was progressing on her bereavement journey.

If we stop on our journey, physical distress may take over all the more. The physical stresses are built-in reminders to urge us to move on. Those of us who are bereaved in the later years can expect to have more physical ailments. It's as if our aging bodies felt the impact of our loss more and had less strength to handle it. This doesn't mean we can't. It means the physical distress may be more prolonged and more difficult than that of younger people.

We may experience sleeplessness. In their book *Up from Grief,* Bernadine Kries and Alice Pattie tell us that "the nights will be long and tortuous. You will awaken hearing sobs. They will be your own. If you are widowed, you will awaken with an arm outstretched, reaching for the unreachable." A major loss, such as the death of our beloved, may cause physical reactions. There can be dizziness, blurred vision, rashes, palpitations, chest pains, shortness of breath, general aching, heavy menstrual periods, fainting, indigestion, and other symptoms.

We can expect much when we are thrust into grief. We can do something, too. A physical examination and medication may be appropriate. But the primary thing we can do is to get on with our bereavement journey. As one person put it, "I was amazed. As I continued to talk, sharing my memories, my feelings, my fears, my hopes, with someone who cared, I sensed my attitude slowly changing. I guess I finally buried my husband. I don't mean physically, but I inwardly 'laid him to rest.' As I spiritually left the graveyard, having really entrusted him to God, I felt more at ease. I started to look at life again. I began to feel better physically. My medicine helped, but I was able to stop taking it. I really believe it was my changing attitude that helped me physically as well as spiritually."

### ∾ Scripture Meditation: Matthew 11:28

"Come to me, all you that are weary and are carrying heavy burdens, and I will give you rest."

*Grant me the courage to see myself as a whole person in your sight, O Lord. Help me to see your message for me, even when it comes to me through my body. I am your creation: body, mind, and soul. Amen.*

# I Can't Go On

*A small animal caught in a trap waits for the unknown,* frightened about what the next minute may bring. It may have struggled to get free when first caught, but the struggle only tightened the trap's grip. Now there is no more struggle, only hopeless resignation and helplessness.

Helplessness is a feeling we have as we anxiously wait for the report of medical tests. Will it be good news? Will it be bad news? Will it be mixed news? There isn't a thing we can do to change the helplessness of this waiting; nor can we speed up, slow down, or alter its results. As much as we try to remain optimistic, hopeful, and in fair spirits, there is no denying this anxious helplessness.

Losing a beloved person can bring on a similar feeling of helplessness. One person remarked that he could no longer go on living without his spouse. He felt helpless and incapacitated. There seemed to be no reason to live.

Feelings of helplessness are intensified by a lack of purpose or reason for living. Even though we feel as if we had no choice about our loss, but are helplessly stuck, we have made a choice. Our movement from helplessness to helpfulness largely depends on choices we make, although it doesn't seem that way. We did not choose our loss. But we do choose to have this loss control us if we don't go on living for ourselves, without our loved one. We can tell when this forward movement begins. From "I can't go on" to "I won't go on" is a giant step.

I was often told, "There is no such word as *can't*." What did this mean? I began to realize that this was a backhanded attempt to motivate me. In other words, *can't* is the choice I make when I refuse to do anything. "No such word as *can't*" was a parental reminder that I have the God-given power to choose otherwise. It is a beautiful moment in our lives when we say, "I didn't want to go on. In fact, I didn't feel able, but now I want to. I realize I can and I will. I can choose to remain helpless, or I can choose to be helpful to myself." Then we who have suffered loss through death can say, "That's what my loved one would want me to do."

I think of Moses at the beginning of his mission. In answer to God's call to be his leader, Moses said, "I can't do it." But the Lord kept knocking down Moses' resistance. The Lord said, "Go, I will help you." It took persistence, even emphatic insistence, on the part of God. Moses finally made the move from "I can't" to "I won't" to "I will." And he did!

God helps us to help ourselves in our helplessness.

## Scripture Meditation: Romans 8:14-15

For all who are led by the Spirit of God are children of God. For you did not receive a spirit of slavery to fall back into fear, but you have received a spirit of adoption.

*Dear God, it's no fun feeling helplessly stuck, yet I could stay this way and sadly like it. But the world doesn't need another immovable rock. I need a shove to start rolling. I believe I can move if you give me an encouraging nudge. Amen.*

# Here, But Gone

*"There was a river separating us.* I could look across the river to the other side. I've never seen anything so beautiful in all my life. I can't describe it. It must have been heaven. Then I saw my son looking across the river at me. It was dark and foggy where I stood, but the sun was shining on him. He said to me, 'It's all right. I'm OK. Don't worry. I'm happy.' Then he turned and walked away into the sun."

This was one of a series of dreams a mother experienced when she lost her 24-year-old son. No one could talk her out of the reality of these dreams. No one should. This dream, with the others, had significance and meaning. It was the God-given unconscious part of her that was speaking in language plain yet mysterious.

Our dreams and visions may carry great and religious meaning. Dreams are sometimes helpful emissaries, friends to aid our bereavement journey. They speak to reality, to pain, to wishes, to fears, to unfinished and unfulfilled needs, to hope.

John Sanford has called the dream "God's forgotten language."

The bereaved mother explained what the dream meant to her. She felt that her son was reassuring her, attempting to nurture and protect her. Prior to his death he was depressed and his life was not going well. This dream place was beautiful. The sun was warm and life was new. He was encouraging her to try harder to let him go.

The friendly dream was helping her to accept her son's death. The fact that she was on the foggy, dark side indicated to her the reality of the dark experience of her loss. She was still in the fog of grief. Not all the work had been completed so that she could stand in the light of her new day. But God was at work.

Many persons have also experienced visions of the dead person standing close to them. Some people have seen the ones who died doing something that they would have done when they were alive. It's as if the death never happened. Eventually, however, the pleasure of the vision or dream gives way to the sad awakening of the loss through death.

Dreams and visions are important. We can see this in the Bible. Joseph gained position and prestige through his visions, dreams, and interpretations. The visions of Daniel are colorful and intriguing conveyors of messages. Our Lord's birth was announced to Joseph in a dream. In our dreams God may have helpful and meaningful messages of challenge, acceptance, hope, and new birth. We may need help to understand these messages, but we can be sure that we are befriended by God in many and mysterious ways.

### Scripture Meditation: 1 Peter 1:3

Blessed be the God and Father of our Lord Jesus Christ! By his great mercy he has given us a new birth into a living hope through the resurrection of Jesus Christ from the dead.

*God, it's only a dream! Or is it? Help me, Lord, to understand what you are saying to me through my dreams. In my journey I need help accepting death and learning to go on living. Amen.*

# Here and Nowhere

*Mr. Wright put his head in his hands while his body convulsed with sobbing.* The crying was painful, choking, burning. He was feeling the wrenching terror of his loneliness.

Mrs. Hayes showed me through her home, a small, ordinary house one passes by without looking twice. Why the tour? Mrs. Hayes' husband had died, and she wanted me to know what he had been and done. She also wanted to share her loneliness without calling it by that name. She pointed out his carpentry work and tools, the pickles and beans they had canned together, the porch room he had built, his couch where he had watched TV, their garden. As she spoke, her lips quivered, her eyes glistened, and her body froze for a moment. It was a courageous and painful work of mourning. Her loneliness spilled over in her eyes and her voice as she reminisced.

There is no way to avoid loneliness completely, and it is better not to try, for the very terror of loneliness also contains the sensitivity of being human. Clark Moustakas has said, "To love is to be lonely. . . . All love leads to suffering. If we did not care for others in a deep and fundamental way, we would not experience grief . . . when they are ill and dying."

Mrs. King was a small, thin woman whose husband had died and left her a widow at the age of 50. She was also a deaf-mute. For many days she wouldn't eat much, seemed despondent, and preferred to sleep away time. It took great effort for her to talk through an interpreter about her husband. Once she began using her sign language, her little body, which was curled in a sitting position, began to unravel. It was hard. Laced through this grief of inaudible words were threads and shreds of loneliness. The years they had spent together, sometimes with more bad times than good, still formed a relationship, which when broken by death created a loneliness never to be totally taken away. Talking about her deep loneliness by talking about her husband and their relationship diminished the hold it had on her. But we knew there was no way to take it all away. One can go on when loneliness is faced, but it remains a shadowy companion.

When we risk facing our loneliness, we may discover new confidence to continue our journey of self-restoration toward meaningful living. By meeting our loneliness we encounter a potential growth experience. No one can do it for us. Loneliness leaves its calling card in our hearts and on our faces, but it can enhance our dignity and maturity and open new possibilities for tenderness.

One day Mr. Sanborn looked at his suffering loneliness and decided he would walk with it. He would be its partner rather than its victim. So he sat down and began to write. He was no writer, he thought, but slowly and falteringly, with words scribbled out and scribbled in, he began to write about his wife and about their life together. His writing, done with his partner, loneliness, at his side, turned out to be a beautiful memoir of his wife and of their life together. He found himself speaking and relating to other people in honest and tender ways. He was rediscovering life, people, and meaning.

Clark Moustakas put it well: "Let there be loneliness, for where there is loneliness, there is also love, and where there is suffering, there is also joy."

### ∽ Scripture Meditation: John 14:16-17

And I will ask the Father, and he will give you another Advocate, to be with you forever. This is the Spirit of truth, whom the world cannot receive, because it neither sees him nor knows him. You know him, because he abides with you, and he will be in you.

*Dear Lord and Father, I didn't choose to be lonely. Loneliness came my way and forced itself on me. People don't always understand, but your Son, my Lord Jesus, knew what it was to be lonely. Help me to accept my loneliness so that I may allow it to move me toward people and life. Be my courage and strength, O God. Amen.*

 # You'll Never Know

*St. Augustine said, "All this grief, my heart was utterly darkened . . .* I was miserable and without joy." Pain and despair are threads that run through us as we move through our journey of bereavement. How many times haven't we said or heard, "The dead have it made. At least they have peace, but I'm left with the suffering. Sometimes I feel I'd rather be dead than alive. At least I wouldn't have to face all this!"

In pain and despair we can echo the words of the old spiritual, "Nobody knows the trouble I've seen. Nobody knows my sorrow." We may have been moving through our journey slowly, doing well, when suddenly the reality of our loss, this death, hits again! There is no going back, no recapturing or retrieving what was lost. Our loved one is gone. The pain invades and grips, and the fullness we were beginning to feel seeps out. Emptiness takes over. The wound opens wide, and we despair. It's as if all life stops again.

Mr. and Mrs. Johnson had spent 64 years together as husband and wife. Sixty-four years! That in itself seems like a lifetime! Just before their sixty-fourth wedding anniversary, Mrs. Johnson was taken to the hospital with what seemed to be a bout with one of those unnamed viruses. Mr. Johnson remained at her bedside. One afternoon, in the course of normal nursing care, the nurse asked him to step out of the room. Moments later, when he reentered, he met not life but death. His wife had quickly and quietly died.

Mr. Johnson's life had been bound up with his wife. The more we have our lives bound up with one another, the more vulnerable we become. So it was with Mr. Johnson. The shock, disbelief, and guilt over having been so close—a few steps away—and yet so far apart, eventually gave way to painful despair. His beloved wife had silently been cut out of his life by death.

One doesn't have to be married 64 years to feel the pain and despair of death. It is not time, but our closeness to our loved one that increases our vulnerability and opens us to deeper pain and despair. Yet when we confront our pain and despair and begin to accept the loss, surrendering ourselves to God in our powerlessness, then pain and despair can give way to hope. The unwanted pain can be accepted and transformed. When we accept our pain as our own, suffering can grow into compassion. It's as if the heart opens, and out of sorrow come warmth and joy.

The life and death of each of us has influence on others: "If we live, we live to the Lord, and if we die, we die to the Lord; so then, whether we live or whether we die, we are the Lord's" (Romans 14:8).

## ◯ Scripture Meditation: Psalm 40:1-2

I waited patiently for the Lord;
he inclined to me and heard my cry.
He drew me up from the desolate pit,
out of the miry bog,
and set my feet upon a rock,
making my steps secure.


*Dear Father, time and again I feel the grip of despair and the pangs of pain. My loss is hard to bear and accept. I wonder how I can go on. I pray, and I'm not sure that you hear. My despair gets the best of me. I remember Jesus' despair on the cross. You heard your Son in that dark moment. Even when I doubt, you do hear me. Help me, Father. Amen.*

# I Know

*You talk about your problem with a friend,* who says, "Yes, I know what you mean." Yet the feeling you get is that this person doesn't know.

We too may have let these words spill out of our mouths. We may have been trying hard to understand another person and wanted that person to know that we were feeling with him.

But there really is no way to know another person's experience of loss and grief. Each of us is unique, and our experience is truly our own. Yet some people come close to knowing our bereavement experience. They somehow convey that they really walk with us in our loss. Perhaps they have experienced a loss like ours. It helps if these people are ones who sensitively know what we may be going through, but don't use our grief as an occasion to talk solely about their own grief and bereavement.

When we lose someone we love, we are uncertain. We may really wonder whether anyone knows what our loss feels like and means to us. Some people are able to turn our doubtfulness into the certainty that someone does know. At that point we feel assured and buoyed.

I recall a man who lost a young son in a tragic accident. At the funeral home people came to give their sympathy, concern, and support. This father had the feeling that most of the people were indeed being kind and concerned in a most uncomfortable and unsettling situation. They didn't really know what to say except the usual clichés and the expected sympathetic talk. He felt their uncomfortableness and their sincerity, but the words were common and cold.

During the funeral home visitation period, one man came into the room, went to the casket, and walked toward the bereaved father. He said nothing. He simply looked into the father's eyes for a few moments, touched him on the shoulder, and left. Not one word was spoken, but a well of wordless messages had flowed.

Later the bereaved father said, "There were many kind people, but they didn't know what to say. I know from all the people who came that they cared. But there was one person who really spoke to me. He didn't say anything. He didn't have to. I knew by his look and his manner that he knew what I was experiencing." This person, too, had lost a child through death.

That was an "I know" meeting of two hearts. It brought assurance. Words aren't always necessary when the heart knows. Doubt is turned into certainty, and this brings comfort in the middle of pain.

### ∞ Scripture Meditation: John 10:14-15

"I am the good shepherd. I know my own and my own know me, just as the Father knows me and I know the Father. And I lay down my life for the sheep."

*Dear God, I have moments when I'm not sure anyone knows what I'm going through. I want to believe someone knows. What I need even more is to realize that you know. Help me to think about your Son, O God. If I think about Jesus, I'll believe that you do know me in my pain. Amen.*

# A Swinging Pendulum

*I once rode a ferry boat to Martha's Vineyard* off the Massachusetts coast. Though it was a large secure boat, I found myself moving up and down, leaning first to one side, then to the other. There was no way to feel still and stable, centered. No matter what I did, I was controlled by the rising and falling of sea waves and by the boat's listing.

After the death of her husband, Wilma felt like a clock's pendulum. Her emotions moved from one side to the other. She felt wound up, and her feelings were in constant motion. She said, "There seem to be at least two of everything in me. I feel caught between opposites. I feel the loss of Bert and it hurts me. Then I feel relieved he's gone. If he had had to be laid up, inactive and suffering, he wouldn't have liked that. I'm not sure I could have taken it either. So sometimes I wish he were here, and then I'm relieved he's not."

She went on, "Some days I remember the good times and a few of the not-so-good times we had together. Other days I want to forget and can't.

Then I think, maybe I ought to sell the place and move; my son says I can come and stay with him. But I look at the place and say, 'No, I'll just stay here.' That's not all. There are times when I want Bert to depend on. I don't like having to do everything he used to do. Before you knew it, though, I learned how to do the things he used to do, and I even like some of that responsibility. In fact, my independence lets me do as I will.

"I'm probably going to get a job like I wanted. When Bert was alive, he didn't want me to work. You see, one minute I want to be dependent and the next minute I like my independence."

Wilma was experiencing some of the opposites of bereavement. Unsettling as this is, it indicates movement in the bereavement journey. Out of these tensions comes energy that helps us to accept our loss and embrace our future. Coming to terms with the opposites we experience within us helps us find ourselves. If we lean only one way, we may be impeding our bereavement journey. Opposites together make something whole.

There is no day without night, no peace without war, no love without hate, no hope without despair, no resurrection without death. As we move between our opposites, we can pray the words of an old hymn:

"Jesus, Savior, pilot me
Over life's tempestuous sea;
Unknown waves before me roll,
Hiding rock and treacherous shoal;
Chart and compass come from thee,
Jesus, Savior, pilot me."

### ∾ Scripture Meditation: Isaiah 58:11

The Lord will guide you continually,
and satisfy your needs in parched places,
and make your bones strong;
and you shall be like a watered garden,
like a spring of water,
whose waters never fail.

*Move with me and in me, O God. As I work toward being myself and coming to a new wholeness in life without my loved one, be my compass and guide, through Jesus Christ, my Lord. Amen.*

# Much Ado

*Most of us want help when we lose a loved one.* But what kind of help do we want, and when?

At the time of death there may have been people who wanted to do everything for us. They may have insisted on calling the relatives and starting funeral arrangements. At home they may have made the coffee, prepared the meals, and helped beyond what was helpful. You may have been one of the number of people who, in spite of appreciation for this help, felt it was too much. As difficult as it was and as grief laden as you may have been, perhaps you felt you could have handled more of the work yourself.

Or maybe you did most of the work yourself. If you did, you were probably coping with the initial shock of your grief.

As time passes, what do we find ourselves doing? How busy and active ought we to be? Tennyson, after the death of his friend Arthur Hallam, wrote: "I must lose myself in action lest I wither in despair."

When the Huffman's son died they moved back and forth between activity and inactivity. There were days when they couldn't concentrate on the smallest task. Mrs. Huffman would begin to write a letter and never finish it. Household work was started and stopped. Sometimes it wasn't even started, but was left neglected. Dust gathered, rugs looked tracked, dishes piled up. Sheets went unchanged, flowers even went unwatered. There seemed to be no energy for anything. Then everything was reversed for a time. The Huffmans felt an overwhelming burst of energy. Activity reached almost a frenzied pitch. Work, work, work! Go, go, go! It was as if they were busy trying to forget. Then their bodies gave way to exhaustion and sleep, but they awakened to the memory of their son's death. It may be that the extremes of all activity or no activity were temporary roadblocks on the bereavement journey.

King David was chastised by Joab, his commander-in-chief, when David found out that his son, Absalom, was dead. David had gone to his room weeping. Joab reprimanded David and told him to "get on with it." Their troops had been victorious. King David and the court were alive. To mourn on a day of victory was shameful. David was to bury his grief, because the people's good came before personal sorrow. This was good military ethics, but doubtful guidance in helping David mourn satisfactorily. David was not the same again. To be forgetful too soon may be an unhelpful denial.

Some of us may feel that we have to get busy. Perhaps well-intentioned people say to us, "Take a trip, visit the relatives, change jobs." We may even think we should sell the house with its well of memories and move away.

Travel may be helpful when we're ready for it, but when it comes to irreversible decisions like moving and selling, it is better to mull it over before we act. We need to work patiently and wait to make decisions. Our impulsive desire to change things may be a momentary need to escape our loss and suffering. We need patience and time to plan helpful and purposeful activity.

### ∞ Scripture Meditation: Isaiah 40:31

But those who wait for the Lord shall renew their strength,
they shall mount up with wings like eagles,
they shall run and not be weary,
they shall walk and not faint.

*Dear God, give me patience and a sense of what helpful activity is for me. Show me when I need to slow down. I don't want to block my journey, but to move onward. Make me aware of your presence in my movement. Amen.*

# Yes

*There are many landmarks in our bereavement journey.* Acceptance is certainly one. In fact, much of our mourning is working toward acceptance. Some of our mourning follows the acceptance of our loved one's death. We begin to reaffirm ourselves in our acceptance of our loss. We may recall how hard it was for the disciples to accept Jesus' prediction of his death. We may also recall the discovery, acceptance, and affirmation of the centurion who stood at the cross and declared, "Truly this man was the Son of God!"

Moving toward acceptance isn't easy. There are days when we feel we have accepted this death, our loss: "Yes, this has happened. It is true." Other days we hedge: "I know it has happened, but it seems too unreal. My head says one thing, and my heart feels something else."

Mr. Bernard said to me following the loss of his wife, "I know she is dead. I must go on without her." The symbol of his finally accepting the loss of his young wife was the gravestone he purchased and placed as his last gift to her. Once he had done that he could inwardly leave the cemetery. His act represented final acceptance of her death.

We live with the acknowledgment that death is in life, without giving it much thought until it hits our lives. If we dwelled on death, we would probably not be living well. But when it hits, we are faced with it. It is no longer the other person, but me! I have lost! We may think we have accepted it, but the disharmony within us and our outer lives and relationships says we really haven't fully accepted it.

I sometimes view older people who seem to go on as being invulnerable. But when an older man I knew died unexpectedly, I couldn't and wouldn't believe it. I had built the illusion that he would go on forever. The fantasies we build make acceptance a slow process.

Mary had accepted her dying and was ready. Jack, her husband, was working at it. Toward the end Mary said good-bye to her husband and family, kissing them and admonishing them to love and care for each other. It was a heart-tearing and beautiful moment. She closed her eyes and slept. Hours later she woke to find she hadn't died and gone to heaven. When she saw all of us she realized death was still eluding her. She was angry. She wanted to die. She had accepted her death. There was no chance for survival. Her body had not reached the point of death, even though her emotions and spirit had reached it. Four days later she died.

Later Jack said, "I had pretty much accepted Mary's death, too. But when she survived after we had said good-bye, I found myself thrown back. The four days were more of what seemed like unnecessary suffering." The interruption indicated how tentative and fragile the initial step of acceptance is.

There is no easy way to accept death. We each must find our own process. We may be helped by good memories, by time, and by expressing our feelings. When our acceptance is coupled with self-affirmation, we have made a great stride. Arlene put her affirmation this way. "John wanted me to go on. As I work to lead my own life without him, I'm really accepting what he gave me, the freedom to be me." What a gift of acceptance!

### ○⃝ Scripture Meditation: Romans 8:38-39

For I am convinced that neither death, nor life, nor angels, nor rulers, nor things present, nor things to come, nor powers, nor height, nor depth, nor anything else in all creation, will be able to separate us from the love of God in Christ Jesus our Lord.

*As Jesus commended his spirit to you, O God, help me to see that my acceptance of this death is the doorway to new life. As death led to resurrection, so lead me to experience the acceptance that brings newness to life. My security is in you, my Father, through Jesus Christ. Amen.*

# Through a Glass Darkly

*"You know, it's a funny thing."* The old gentleman looked pensive. "I don't mean funny in the humorous sense, but it's a strange thing. I think of my Alice quite often. Her death was hard, and I took it hard. I knew it was coming, but death was like a stranger—a stranger you don't really know, even though he's always around." This man was struggling with an unresolvable issue—the mystery of death. Even if death is seen as a result of humanity's fall into sin, it is still a mystery.

In the Old Testament it is death that the person of faith sees as a threat to relationship with God. It was life that was to be felt and experienced in relationship with God. The stranger, death, was the mysterious visitor that could bring this meaningful, covenanted relationship with God to an end.

Jesus did little preaching or teaching about death. He didn't see death as a roadblock to our relationship with God. Jesus emphasized life and its fulfillment. His own death was overcome by his victorious resurrection. Jesus didn't say much about what happened to people after they died, but he promised everlasting life to all who believed in him.

Paul saw death as the enemy, but an enemy defeated by Christ. Death is our foe, but "Thanks be to God, who gives us the victory through our Lord Jesus Christ." We take heart and hope in this resurrection victory.

Marlene Browne said, "For a long time after my mother and then my husband died, I experienced not only bitterness but fear. I was fearful of death, life, the future. Death seemed to squeeze the life out of me. I felt like an empty shell." Marlene fought back, wrestling herself out of this stranglehold of death. The first indication of victory appeared when she became aware that death, the stranger, would be her enemy only as she allowed it to be. She didn't need to be controlled by it. Why? She realized that she was worshiping life for its own sake. The more she worshiped life and her lost relationships, the more death took over.

Then she remembered Mary's encounter with Jesus in the garden. Marlene substituted her name for Mary's and heard Jesus saying, "Woman, why are you weeping?" Then, in her mind, she heard him say, "Marlene!" She began to make the turn from defeat to victory. Death the mystery, became death the door to hope. It was another beginning.

### ∞ Scripture Meditation: 1 Corinthians 15:55-57

"Where, O death, is your victory?
Where, O death, is your sting?"

The sting of death is sin, and the power of sin is the law. But thanks
be to God, who gives us the victory through our Lord Jesus Christ.

*Dear Father, my death and the deaths of people I love are a mystery.
Although I may not give up searching out the mystery, I do want not to torture
myself to know the unknowable. You have penetrated and conquered it. My
hope is in you; I need no more. Your saving grace is enough. Thank you, through
Christ my Lord. Amen.*

# There Is a Season

*The author of Ecclesiastes wrote that* "for everything there is a season, and a time for every matter under heaven: a time to be born, and a time to die." Does that mean that beyond the natural rhythm of life that we see in the change of seasons there is also a rhyme and reason for what occurs? Is there a purpose in the death we've experienced?

To one man, death was no more than the end of life. Death itself meant nothing. Anything purposeful was contained in the life lived. Death was the sword that declared "the end."

On the other hand, there was the woman who said, "Having to face the fact that my husband was dying made us value our love for each other with an intensity and intimacy we had not known before. Every day became a gift to experience together. No longer did we take life or our relationship for granted."

Marge said, "For a long time I couldn't accept the death of my son. I cursed God for snatching this precious life from me! As I let go of my anger and directed my attention to my two remaining children, I made a discovery.

My relationship to my children and my husband began to grow in a way I hadn't experienced before. My husband and I went through an agonizing period that nearly ended in divorce. But we worked at our feelings and relationship with the help of others. Out of the ashes of our loss and conflict came a new life, a new commitment to our marriage." They moved out from themselves toward mutual involvement in church and charity work, particularly with other parents who had experienced the death of a child. They grew in personal maturity, marital fidelity, and intimacy. Was this caused by their child's death? They would say that since their tragic loss, their lives had taken on new meaning and value.

In Christ, life is intended to have purpose. Perhaps we all too easily become worshippers of life. We may make life itself into an idol. If all our marbles are in a basket called *life,* death may indeed be the unwanted, purposeless intruder. This is not to say we shouldn't "have life and have it abundantly," as Jesus said. But to make anything, including life, into the "be all and end all," squeezes God out of the picture. It is our relationship with God in life that enables us to make sense out of seeming nonsense. Even when sense and purpose seem to escape us, we trust that one day we will understand. On that day we will come face to face with the author of life.

A courageous statement was made by a person who, in struggling to understand the death of his beloved, said, "I still do not see the purpose. I struggle, but I don't give up. Somehow I feel that in my very struggle with this I am choosing to say that there is purpose and meaning." Giving up may mean the quiet desperation of despair. There is wisdom in the search and struggle.

When Jesus met Martha, she said to him, "If you had been here, my brother would not have died." Jesus answered, "I am the resurrection and the life. Those who believe in me, even though they die, will live, and everyone who lives and believes in me will never die. Do you believe this?"

### ∾ Scripture Meditation: Lamentations 3:31-33

For the Lord will not reject forever.
Although he causes grief, he will have compassion
according to the abundance of his steadfast love;
for he does not willingly afflict or grieve anyone.

*Lord, I do believe. Accept my times of doubt and feelings of purposelessness. Help me understand your purpose for my life. Guide me in my search for personal truth. Hear my prayer, O Lord. Amen.*

# Those Old Feelings

*"Sometimes I felt guilty for even feeling my own sexual desires.* I suppose I tried not to think of sex, you know what I mean . . . I felt maybe it was un-Christian. I guess I just didn't think about my sexual life for awhile. I don't think I wanted to. I was preoccupied with other concerns and with my wife's memory. I felt it might be almost violating my love for my wife. She died almost ten months ago. I don't feel that way as much as I did a few months back."

Some Christians are able to discuss sexuality freely and openly. Others feel that to talk about sex borders on the sinful, yet our sexuality is a real and God-given part of us.

It is good for us to deal with our sexuality as part of our bereavement journey. How can we simply ignore something that has been a vital part of our relationship? When a loved one dies, the relationship to that person, who lives on in us, is as real as if it still existed. If this person was your marriage partner, grief has dulled temporarily the sexual feelings and desires. As these feelings and desires emerge quite naturally from our underground of grief, we have choices to make. It isn't sinful or wrong to have these desires. We aren't being unfaithful to the deceased loved one, even though we may feel as if we were.

Cliff's wife had a cancer that slowly took her life. He gradually started anticipating her death months before it occurred. After she died, Cliff met a woman who had lost her husband, and the two of them eventually married. In fact, they married fairly quickly after meeting. Cliff's children were angry about their father's speedy remarriage and thought it showed no respect to their mother's memory. What they didn't understand was that Cliff had been grieving his wife's death long before she actually died. His children hadn't.

Cliff was also a relational, amorous man who was intensely lonely after his wife's death. He wanted and needed a woman's companionship and love. He didn't see the new marriage as a betrayal of his first wife's memory. They had discussed the subject and encouraged each other to remarry in the event one of them should die. There was no doubt in Cliff's mind that his wife would have done the same thing.

There are those who choose to and can live quite contentedly without sex or marriage after the death of a loved one. Others may find that their sexual desires return after the shock of grief wears off.

God calls us to fullness after our loved one dies, just as he did before the death. Because our sexuality is as individual as our fingerprints, it is more important for some than for others. The point is that in our bereavement journey the rediscovery of sexuality is good. It can be a sign that we are risking making headway toward embracing ourselves, others, and life.

### ∽ Scripture Meditation: 1 John 4:11-12

Beloved, because God loved us so much, we also ought to love one another. No one has ever seen God; if we love one another, God lives in us, and his love is perfected in us.

*Lord, it sometimes isn't easy to think about my sexuality, let alone to talk to you about it. I'm not ashamed of being human, but I get uneasy admitting personal and intimate thoughts and feelings. Yet you are my Father. Help me to trust you. In trusting your understanding of me, O God, I can better trust myself. Amen.*

# Reaching and Touching

*"Death ends a life,"* said Robert Anderson, "but it does not end a relationship, which struggles in the survivor's mind toward some resolution, which it never finds." None of us can really erase a meaningful, loving relationship when death closes the door on it. We may not see it, but we know it is there, inside of us; we know it is a part of us.

One man expressed what many feel: "It has been three and one-half months since Marguerite died. I've had many dreams in which she seems to be alive, but morning comes and I am alone in bed. It's been helpful to have so many warm feelings flood over me. I've seen people with whom Marguerite was especially close. I am still seeing people and places through Marguerite's eyes. I remember her soft warmth and I also remember her anger about all the forces in the world which encourage hate, mistrust, and greed, preventing people from living as human beings. I can look back on the past three years and know that our relationship grew and deepened so that these years became the most meaningful of our nearly 28 years together."

Moving forward in our bereavement toward new relationships does not mean the end of the remembered relationship. The old relationship is not meant to hold us back forever, but to help us in engaging in new relationships.

Making this transition differs for each individual. For some of us, old friends may want us to return and to relate to them as we did prior to the death. This can be unfair and unrealistic. It is better for us if we move into relationships that have real meaning and satisfaction for us. These may include our old friends, but may not, in truth, include all of them. One woman told me, "Some of my friends are well meaning, I suppose, but sometimes I wish they would go away and leave me alone. They want me to act like nothing has happened!"

Nancy related: "I let my friends know when I was ready to rejoin them in our flower club. They were a little pushy at first, but I made it clear, 'When I'm ready, you'll know!'" Nancy had her mourning and her relationships well in hand.

One of the most unsettling prospects may be that of establishing a close relationship with a person of the opposite sex. A real platonic friendship is a possibility and a good solution. It is especially good for those of us who have always enjoyed the opposite sex while still maintaining a personal Christian ethic that makes sex without marriage wrong.

A companionship relationship can be a stimulating and fulfilling blessing. This works when we want to share time with the other person without the deep, responsible emotional involvement that love in marriage brings.

Mrs. Michaelson said she had always enjoyed the companionship of her late husband's men friends. In fact, she said, "My husband was the kind of man who was glad I could enjoy the company of his friends. They knew our relationship wasn't sexual, but simply a good and interesting friendship." Mrs. Michaelson continued, "I now occasionally see a few of these men." They continued the meaningfulness of their relationships. No marriage was intended, just platonic friendship. This may not be usual for most of us. Yet it can be a valuable help in the process of affirming ourselves and other people.

If you contemplate and struggle with the possibility of remarriage, you may find the words of Joseph C. Landrud helpful: "The way out of this seeming impasse is to return in meditation to the *memory* of our love relationship with the departed. Was that love relationship truly free, spontaneous, self-giving, and life-affirming? If so, it is no healthy testimony to the quality of our love for someone to say that when he or she died our ability to love also died. Authentic love which, in its deepest form is the love of God expressed through us to all, without limit and without end, could certainly find a new object in the world around us. It is this deep and limitless love that truly makes us free."

Whether we contemplate remarriage or not, it is important to embrace some people in relationships that give meaning and vitality. Our bereavement journey is not one of separation, but one that steadily moves toward people.

### ∽ Scripture Meditation: 1 Corinthians 13:1-2

If I speak in the tongues of mortals and of angels, but do not have love, I am a noisy gong or a clanging cymbal. And if I have prophetic powers, and understand all mysteries and all knowledge, and if I have all faith, so as to remove mountains, but do not have love, I am nothing.

*Dear God, give me courage to reach within and to reach out. Lessen my fear to touch the lives of others. Enable me to receive and to give, like Jesus, your Son and my Lord. Amen.*

# Constant Care

*"At first you did not love enough; and afterwards you loved too much."* These lines from Stephen Spender may express the deeply felt but seldom spoken refrain haunting those of us who feel we loved too much: "If we hadn't loved each other so much, hadn't been so close, maybe I wouldn't hurt so now. I can't let go, and I can't go on."

This love of ours has lost its intended receiver. Although there is no longer responding love, the memories of our relationship and of our love together remain with us, etched permanently into our being. We keep these etchings even as we journey forward. Edith Sitwell has said, "Love is not changed by death and nothing is lost and all in the end is harvest."

A pastor in Wisconsin who had lost his wife to cancer expressed some of his "love etchings" this way. "We believed in God, but realized that our faith did not guarantee us any special treatment of length of days. The quiet touch of hands as we watched a sunset over Lake Mendota, or the eager excitement as we watched thousands of geese come into Horicon Marsh, or a quiet dinner with friends, each took on a special depth of meaning, which was felt, but hard to realize."

A mother who had lost her son said that her love for him would never die. "All my love wasn't wrapped only in my son. He will be with me as part of me, but my love will not be limited; it never has been." Her love knew no rigid perimeters. It was flowing out to touch others. In this love she reached beyond death into life.

The floods of mourning cannot drown the force of love that reaches beyond the grave. Love lives beyond death, into resurrection. Love cares, reaches out, gives, feeds. It goes beyond the self and even beyond our loved one. Nothing, not even death itself, can ultimately separate us from the love in Christ Jesus our Lord. Death has been conquered. Love is freed to flow.

### ∾ Scripture Meditation: Philippians 3:20-21

But our citizenship is in heaven, and it is from there that we are expecting a Savior, the Lord Jesus Christ. He will transform the body of our humiliation that it may be conformed to the body of his glory, by the power that also enables him to make all things subject to himself.

*May my memories be a living love. May my loving be more than a memory. O God, grant me the assurance that death has lost its sting in the victorious love of my resurrected Lord. In that name of Jesus Christ, I pray. Amen.*

# Springs in the Desert

*The desert wanderer moves on in the hope* to find an oasis with water and shade to sustain and fortify life. There may be periods of parchedness in our bereavement journey when we, too, long for "a spring in the desert"—times of dryness that seem to push us toward hopelessness. To give hope to the discouraged people of his time, Isaiah used that same image of a spring in describing the blessing that was to come through God's Savior.

Included in his hope-giving vision was the promise that "waters shall break forth in the wilderness, and streams in the desert; the burning sand shall become a pool, and the thirsty ground springs of water."

Having a future that reaches beyond the death of our loved one requires hope. Hope belongs to life and reaches beyond death. According to the Bible, we don't create hope, but we receive it from God.

Jim Meyer said, "While my son was dying, my wife and I searched frantically and hopefully for a cure. We never lost the hope that something would be discovered that would yet save our son. After he died we still kept aware of any developments that might have helped our son but that now would be of help to other people dying from cancer." Jim said, "This hope is important. When I realized that the chances of my son being the recipient of a new cure were becoming fewer and fewer, I became more realistic about it, but the glimmer of hope was always there." Hope was sustaining to him and his wife.

After the death, hope took on another dimension. It now became a matter of having a future. It became a matter of "meaningful survival," a survival that would expand into fulfilling and meaningful relationships. Jim described his hope as coming to him as a gift. "I played a part. I had to struggle, but I felt God was at work creating it in me through my bereavement struggle. I found myself reviewing and renewing my relationship to my other three children. I began to see that the future I needed to embrace centered around the meaningfulness of my life with my wife and family. I had really neglected them."

The loss of his loved one actually pushed him toward those he loved. The dryness of his loss led to springs of rebirth in his surviving relationships. He went on to say, "Perhaps hope reaches beyond death into life and relationships in this way."

There was one more way. Jim's hope was for now and for the future. His hope was in Jesus Christ, who would one day come to reunite and make new. In Christ was the eternal hope that became a vital part of Jim's thoughts of his future in life and in death. Isaac Watts put it this way:

O God, our help in ages past,
Our hope for years to come;
Be thou our guide while life shall last,
And our eternal home.

## ∾ Scripture Meditation: 1 Thessalonians 4:13-14

But we do not want you to be uninformed, brothers and sisters, about those who have died, so that you may not grieve as others do who have no hope. For because we believe that Jesus died and rose again, even so, through Jesus, God will bring with him those who have died.

*Hope springs eternal even when I'm unaware. As water gushes beneath the surface, unseen, your gift of hope is there for me. Help me to tap it for new life. In it is the Spirit, pointing to my eternal home where my loved one also dwells. Amen.*

# The Prized Possession

*In the letter to the Philippians, Paul says,* "For I have learned, in whatever state I am, to be content." Paul wasn't talking about grief or the mourning process, but what he says is significant for our bereavement. "Whatever state I am in" could apply to all the life crises you and I experience, certainly including the death of our loved one. "I have learned . . . to be content" indicates that the contentment of peace doesn't always just happen, or come to us suddenly without our working at it.

Some people may have experienced a peace that seemed to fill them unexpectedly. A man told me about the death of his father: "I drove to the small country church where my father's funeral service was held. I sensed the quietness of the countryside, the beauty of the woods I passed, the warmth of that summer day. I felt a dawning peace begin to break within me. In a matter of seconds I felt this peace come all over me." The man was at peace with death and the loss of his father.

For many of us peace is something that grows gradually within us. With Paul we learn to become content with our loss. A young couple lost their eight-year-old daughter, who died from leukemia. In their bereavement process they reached a point of acceptance, which brought them peace. They put it this way: "We have come to the conclusion that we regret nothing with Anne. At first we regretted all the years we wouldn't have with her, all the years she wouldn't have to grow and experience life and become a woman with a life and future. She didn't have that, and we didn't have that with her. But we've experienced to the full those eight years we had together. No, eight years for Anne and for us were a lifetime. We're thankful for eight years, and we're learning to be at peace."

This couple did something that may be hard yet instructive for us. They began to measure life not by the number of years, as we and society easily do, but by the quality of life each of us is privileged to have. They realized that it isn't how many years we have as much as what we are and do within those years that is important. In making this major movement in attitude they found peace.

The peace that some of us may come to is simply the inner knowledge that, "Yes, my loved one and I are safe in Jesus' keeping."

Words always fall short of expressing exactly the inner certainty and comfort of peace. We acknowledge this when we say: "The peace of God, which passes all understanding, keep your hearts and minds through Christ Jesus."

**∞ Scripture Meditation: Psalm 23:1-2**

The Lord is my shepherd, I shall not want.
He makes me lie down in green pastures;
he leads me beside still waters;
he restores my soul.

*Encourage us, O Lord, to find peace in the full realization of our loss. Strengthen us in the faith that peace isn't an elusive dream, but a heartfelt reality that comes after a hard-fought journey. As Jesus came to peace with the words, "It is finished," help us to come to the point in our pilgrimage when we, too, can say, "It is completed." Amen.*

# A Mustard Seed

*"If only I had more faith, I'd feel better.* I'd be able to handle myself in this situation." How much faith is enough in our mourning? Some of us feel that it is always more than what we have. Jesus said that the amount of faith isn't important: "For truly I tell you, if you have faith the size of a mustard seed, you will say to this mountain, 'Move from here to there,' and it will move; and nothing will be impossible for you" (Matthew 17:20).

A grain of mustard seed! Do you recall how small a mustard seed is? Necklaces used to be worn with a mustard seed in the bulb, which magnified it so that it could be seen with normal eye sight. Now if we have faith, though it be that small, nothing will be impossible.

I interpret faith in this instance as basic trust. We don't need a huge quantity of it in order to get on with our bereavement. In fact, if we worry about having a lot of faith, we may miss the mustard seed we do have.

Our mustard seed faith will help us move the mountain of grief. Peggy said, "I have often become discouraged trying to work through my grief. I still feel like giving up sometimes. I wonder if I'm going to make it, and ask

'How long is this going to take?' Then something in me says, 'Peggy, you can do it. Don't give up.' I feel some kind of trust, and I keep going. That little spark gives me confidence to try. I have life ahead of me, even though it's not the same." Peggy was, in her own way, talking about her experience with the mustard seed faith.

The giver of this grain of faith is God, whose Son, though despondent and despairing in his crisis, maintained his faith. He went through his Gethsemane of grief with the word "Father" still on his lips.

We, too, can go through the valleys and mountains of our bereavement journey with "Father" on our lips. Our hearts may wonder, doubt, and cry out in pain, but these feelings will not obliterate our faith. Even when we think we have lost that mustard seed, we do well to remember that our Father is faithful, for he has loved us first.

### ✑ Scripture Meditation: Matthew 9:20-22

Then suddenly a woman who had been suffering from hemor-rhages for twelve years came up behind him and touched the fringe of his cloak, for she said to herself, "If I only touch his cloak, I will be made well." Jesus turned, and seeing her he said, "Take heart, daughter, your faith has made you well." And instantly the woman was made well.

*O God, help me to trust in and through the shadows of my grief. A small seed can do so much. It can split the mountains of my grief and create new life. Amen.*

# Forget Me Not

*Nicholas Wolterstorff, a professor of philosophy* at Calvin College in Michigan, lost his twenty-five-year-old son, Eric, in a mountain-climbing accident. In his book *Lament for a Son* (Grand Rapids, Mich.: Eerdmans, 1987), Wolterstorff writes, "Suddenly here he is again. The chain of suggestion can begin almost anywhere: a phrase heard in a lecture, an unpainted board on a house, a lamp pole, a stone. From such innocuous things my imagination winds its sure way to my wound. Everything is charged with the potential of a reminder. There's no forgetting."

"There's no forgetting" rings in the ears and strikes in the heart. He is right. You and I know that. The loss of a loved one isn't something consigned to a memory dust heap—something we sweep away never to be thought about again. Yet, if I've heard it once, I've heard it too often: "In time, you will forget." I still don't like hearing that phrase. I certainly don't agree with it. I believe it is anti-grief and meant to ease the speaker's feelings of helplessness and discomfort.

The phrase takes different forms: "Time heals; before you know it, you won't think much about it." "Thank God we have been given the ability to forget." All variations on this theme amount to the same message: "Forget it. You will be better off."

The truth is, we don't forget, and we won't be better off trying to do so.

There will be times when we need temporarily to forget or deny our loss, simply in order to deal with the pain. But, as we work through our unique journey of grief, we also will do much remembering. A combination of temporary forgetfulness and vivid memories can teach us how to remember differently.

Trudy said there were days when she wouldn't think about Ned. Then something like the dog barking at 5:30 p.m. would startle her into thinking that he was home from work. She would long to hear his voice. Such feelings of longing might linger for up to half an hour. But gradually she learned to tell herself that "No, he will not be home again." She said she found herself telling Max, the dog, "No, Max, Ned's not home. I miss him, too."

Think what it would mean if we were truly to forget. We would also lose those memories that hug us in warmth, engage us with wistful sighs, and occasionally shake us in laughter. The wonderfully special experiences we had with our loved one would be lost, too. Even the memories of conflicts and difficult times—which we may indeed want to forget—are part of the totality of what we knew and meant to each other. As one person said, "I want to remember it all, warts and beauty marks—the whole package, so to speak."

The best advice is "Do not try to forget." Memories are good. And in time, our struggles with grief will help us learn how to remember—and may even surprise us with what our memories recall.

The words from a eucharistic prayer (From *All Our Losses/All Our Griefs*, Kenneth Mitchell and Herbert Anderson. Louisville: Westminster, 1983, p. 131) remind us that remembering can lead to thanksgiving, and when that happens, our memories are indeed cherished: "Remembering therefore . . . his life-giving passion and death, his glorious resurrection and ascension, and the promise of his coming again, we give thanks to Thee, Lord God Almighty."

### ∾ Scripture Meditation: Psalm 22:27

All the ends of the earth shall remember
and turn to the Lord;
and all the families of the nations
shall worship before him.

*Dear Father, be ever present in my thoughts and memories. Teach me how to remember with a full heart and with thanksgiving. Amen.*

# To Tell the Old, Old Story

*In her beautifully moving book* about the loss of her son, *Andrew, You Died Too Soon,* Corinne Chilstrom describes her experiences with others who have lost a loved one. She writes: "I often approach a grieving person by asking . . . 'What is the heaviest, hardest thing you are dealing with right now?' Grievers know, and they are often quick to respond. We grievers can tell you. And we will, if we believe that you won't judge us and that you really care. You'll be a messenger from God for us. If you will listen, you will lighten our burden, relieve our stress, and our health will be better for your ministry to us."

So I ask *you,* "What is the heaviest, hardest thing you are dealing with right now?"

Have you been asked such a question lately by someone who truly cared, who truly wanted to listen? If so, you are fortunate indeed. You and I need to tell and retell our old, yet ever-new story of grief.

In many situations, we may need to seek out someone who is willing to listen. That usually isn't easy. People are often uncomfortable because they don't know what to say or how to act around a grieving person. Sometimes this means that we need to establish an ongoing relationship with a minister or even a counselor or therapist.

Often, however, the problem is caused by our shyness and reluctance to impose on others. Sometimes those who have been through losses can sense others who need to talk. When they are ready and have their own grief in hand, these people can be listening ministers. But often, if we don't ask, nobody will know our needs.

Greta said that she had about three or four people who would listen to her. She tried not to wear out their friendship and their ears. She said she noticed that, as she told and retold her grief story, she would remember more things to add. As the story was repeated over and over, Greta noticed how the tenses of her verbs eventually began to change. She said, "When I heard myself talking about Kurt with 'was, used to, had been,' I knew I was moving along and better accepting my loss. I had to tell my stories over and over though before I realized that I was really getting along in my grief."

As they listen to our stories again and again, some people may hear only repetitions of the same thing. Truly caring listeners, though, will begin to notice all kinds of subtle differences and changes and realize that we are moving through our grief.

It is often difficult for us to include everything in our grief stories. We tend to be selective, to tell only what is positive and good. Talking about conflicts and difficulties with our loved one may be wrenching. However, we do no one any good by making our relationship with our loved one into something more than it was, by making our loved ones into saints.

Our stories carry us along on a very human journey in which we need to recall the bad as well as the good. We don't have to apologize for this. We simply need to tell it like it was and is. Difficult as this may seem, our stories must be true and complete. And in those shivering moments when we hear ourselves being brutally honest, we can be comforted by the assurance that God takes his coat of acceptance and grace and wraps us up like a best friend would do.

### ∾ Scripture Meditation: Psalm 130:7-8

O, Israel, hope in the Lord!
for with the Lord there is steadfast love,
and with him is great power to redeem.
It is he who will redeem Israel
from all its iniquities.

*Dear God, as I hear the refrain of the old hymn, "I Love to Tell the Story," help me to tell my story and to find those people who will listen to my refrain of joy and pain. As I tell my story, may I also remember and be held by the story of Jesus and his love for me. Amen.*

# Suffering and New Life

*I once heard a professor explain* that he regularly surveyed his college students about times when they felt most alive. Many gave expected answers such as "When I'm surrounded by friends" or "When I have as much money as I can get." A couple of answers came back that startled him. Several students answered that they felt most alive when they experienced pain or suffering.

Think about that response for a minute. Does it seem crazy to you? The very thing that most of us spend our lives trying to eliminate or minimize—suffering—is viewed as the source for feelings of vitality and life. Even our religion is often seen as a way to avoid or reduce suffering.

The Christian mystic, Meister Eckhart, once said, "It is in the darkness that one finds the light, so when we are in sorrow, then this light is nearest to all of us."

"I didn't really know what I had until I lost it." "Funny, he's been dead for four years, but in some ways he seems more alive to me now than ever." "Now that he's gone, I don't take a lot of things for granted that I used to." "There are things we used to do that we both appreciated; these seem more meaningful to me now that she has passed away." All of these statements by people who have lost a loved one imply that their suffering has made life somehow more rich and meaningful.

It is ironic and seemingly paradoxical that the deep suffering that comes with our loss—the times when the darkness of the soul seems to wrap us too tightly—often sit side by side with times when our loss seems to have strangely enriched our lives. There are moments when we see more clearly, imagine more vividly, even experience a mysterious clarity in which we are able to separate the meaningful and life-enhancing from the shallow and trivial. We may experience a deeper valuing of relationships, of nature, of memories. This inner knowing is difficult to explain precisely, but it is very real.

Leila described what she called "strange experiences" that took her a while to explain and accept. One of those experiences involved the hymn "How Great Thou Art," a favorite of both hers and her husbands. After he died, Leila couldn't hear the hymn without floods of tears and a strong desire to stop the hymn, turn it off. As her grief journey continued, she slowly began to orient herself to living again.

She recalled one of many turning points on the journey. Although she still felt some tears when she heard or sang "How Great Thou Art," she also began to sense a deepened appreciation for God's greatness and grace. "Somehow I began to see both nature and the people around me with what

I can call a 'new eye.' I can't explain it, it is so frustrating trying to tell you what this is like. But I know a kind of joy, a kind of excitement that's sometimes even greater than when Jake was living. At first I felt guilty and wanted to deny it. But when it happened again, I began to realize how true this is for me. Then I thought, 'It's okay.' It seems so strange, but my suffering has turned, sometimes, to a kind of joy. I feel so alive again, even in my sadness."

In his book *Lament for a Son* (Grand Rapids, Mich.: Eerdmans, 1987), Nicholas Wolterstorff writes: "Suffering is the shout of 'No' by one's whole existence to that over which one suffers. . . . Sometimes when the cry is intense, there emerges a radiance, which elsewhere seldom appears: a glow of courage, of love, of insight, of selflessness, of faith. In that radiance, we see best what humanity was meant to be."

### ∽ Scripture Meditation: 1 Peter 5:10-11

And after you have suffered for a little while, the God of all grace, who has called you to his eternal glory in Christ, will himself restore, support, strengthen, and establish you. To him be the power forever and ever. Amen.

*O God, I love and I suffer. Move within me in those mysterious ways to help me realize those things that can enrich me without diminishing the realness of my loss or myself. In your gracious name I pray. Amen.*

# Laughter Is Good for the Soul

*Where would we be—who would we be—*without a sense of humor? Some people who have lost a loved one may feel they will never recover a sense of humor. Some people don't want to.

Numerous grieving people and authors of books about illness, stress, and other painful experiences often point to the important role of humor in dealing with the crises of living. It is no less true for those of us who have lost a loved one.

When my father died, my mother, brother, and I decided to have a gathering at my parents' apartment after the funeral. We invited close friends of my parents and the few relatives who had been able to travel the many miles to attend the funeral. The relatives were an aunt and cousins whom I hadn't seen for a number of years. As we ate the donated food, we reminisced and sang some of Dad's and our favorite hymns. With our sharing came rounds of loud laughter salted with tears.

My father and his next younger brother had been both creators and characters of stories. They were the "nix nooses" as kids. They had found great pleasure in recalling and laughing at their childhood escapades and devilry. My uncle had usually been the instigator and my father the passive participant—but a key participant!

The cousins who were at the post-funeral gathering were children of that uncle. Together we reminisced, laughed, cried, hugged, sang, and silently recalled our fathers. It was as close to an Irish wake as a German family could get. It was wonderful! I still smile today as I write about that gathering.

To not have shared that experience—particularly the humor that carried its own kind of tears—would have been a great loss. I look back at how providential that gathering was. It brought pleasure and joy to a painful grief.

For some people, humor emerges later in the grief journey. As we are distanced from the intensity, the loneliness and emptiness, the space can sometimes be partially filled with smiles and laughter. We smile as we recall our loved one's pet quirks or "you'll never believe this" experiences. Even those petty irritations, once so aggravating but now dearly missed, are sometimes transformed into humorous memories.

Martin would smile as he recalled how he and his wife argued about map directions whenever they took a trip in their car. "We were both right, of course. I do hate to admit it, but she was right most of the time!" He chuckled to himself and added, "I said *most of the time!* . . . I guess I am still arguing with her."

Such humor brings laughter, but it also brings sadness as it triggers memories of our loss. The ancient drama masks in which one face exhibits sadness and tears and the other, laughter and joy, reflect the dual reality of our humanness and our grief. Both laughter and tears are mysteriously intertwined in all of life, they are inseparable. And even in our grief there will be moments of healing laughter, occasions to smile.

Humor is part of our life. It was—*is*—also part of the life of our loved one.

I still chuckle out loud when I recall my late uncle's stories about selling fruits and vegetables at a farmer's market in Niagara Falls. One time he couldn't get people to buy his cantaloupes, which were selling for ten cents each in those days. My uncle's blue eyes twinkled as he described how he solved the problem with a sign reading "Two cantaloupes for twenty-five cents." Naturally, he sold them all!

Laugh. Cry. It is all good grief!


### ∾ Scripture Meditation: Psalm 126:5-6

May those who sow in tears
reap with shouts of joy.
Those who go out weeping,
bearing the seed for sowing,
shall come home with shouts of joy,
carrying their sheaves.

*Dear Lord, just as you gave us tear ducts to cry, you gave us ribs and stomachs to shake with laughter. My grief is serious work. I have a need for light and lightness in order to keep my balance. Whatever can help me laugh, even as I cry, I will be thankful for. Give me laughter and joy in my grief. In your name I pray. Amen.*

 # The Community of Faith

*"Here was a group of people who understood my grief.* They listened. They cared. This has been one of the biggest helps to me. It has helped me to live, to reach out of myself to other people. I finally began to crawl out of my protective shell. I didn't find it easy to share my loss. I was ready to give up. I felt no one could ever have gone through what I was going through. But this group of fellow suffering, caring people reached me. I stopped feeling sorry for myself, and I found I could be helpful to some of them. I have really regained faith in myself, my friends, my God, and my church." These are the words of a person who had been involved in a church grief group.

This small group of people met regularly to share their losses with one another. Our bereavement journey is not easily traveled. A group of travelers who share human losses can make the journey a supportive and integrative experience. The church is not only a place in which to thank and praise, but also to share sorrow.

I remember singing an old hymn, "My church, my church, my dear old church." For some of us the church hasn't always been dear. The birth of helping groups, such as grief groups, may rekindle some of the dearness of the gathered community of faith. Perhaps you don't have a group like this in your church. You may be able to start one. No one is a stranger to loss. We are people who experience death and losses within the church community. We aren't alone.

The church, as a community of the faithful, has been at the work of grief, bereavement, binding the brokenhearted, for a long time. The church has been about this before any formal grief group was ever organized. We and people through the centuries have gathered to share confession, absolution, song, prayer, Word and Sacrament, the risen Christ. Gathering to reflect and praise, we come with our grief to have it understood by a grieving Lord who triumphed over the grief of death. Here we experience the Shared Sufferer who can rekindle our faith and help us to come through our darkest hours.

The community of faith stands to continually touch our innermost bereaved self with collective support and the offer of renewed life through the goodness in Jesus Christ, our Lord and Savior.

### ∽ Scripture Meditation: Romans 12:12-15

Rejoice in hope, be patient in suffering, persevere in prayer. Contribute to the needs of the saints; extend hospitality to strangers.

Bless those who persecute you; bless and do not curse them. Rejoice with those who rejoice, weep with those who weep.

*The church's one foundation is Jesus Christ, her Lord. Help me to lean on this Rock that will not crumble, but will support me through grief to life. Amen.*

# What Lies Beyond?

*Speculation and controversy surround our ideas* of what happens after death. There is a great resurgence of interest in what lies beyond the grave.

What I share with you comes from the lives of people who, like us, experienced the death of a loved one and tried to face the absence. They confronted the abyss of death and asked, "What now?" I will not forget the elderly lady who had lived her life wanting to experience everything possible. She had that unusual attitude that led her to risk experiences. She said to me, "I don't want them to stick needles in me, tube me, and do all sorts of things to numb me, push me into unconsciousness, and then keep me alive, without me knowing it." She was firm and angry. "I don't want any of that stuff. I want to experience my own death!"

I asked her, "What then?"

She said, "I've always tried to experience things. I won't be cheated out of experiencing my own death. Then, I don't worry. I'll be in the hands of God, and that's enough for me."

Wilbur told me that he didn't think too much anymore about the afterlife. He felt he would one day see his wife. For him it was enough to know that she had believed and said to him, prior to her death, "I'll be in heaven."

Maggie said she believed her loved one had been reclaimed by his Father, who was her Father, too. "I feel the pain and loss, but I know he's home."

A. J. Gossip's wife died. This Scottish minister had had a companionship with his wife that had been evident to his congregation. When he returned to the pulpit for the first time after his wife's death, his sermon title was, "When Life Tumbles in, What Then?" The closing lines of his sermon on crossing the river of grief would not be forgotten by those who heard him. "I, too, like Hopeful, can call back to you when one day in turn you will have to cross it, 'Be of good cheer my brothers, for I feel the bottom, and it is sound.'"

Search, think, feel, look, ponder, try. Yet, let us take our ultimate assurance in this, "Do not let your hearts be troubled. Believe in God, believe also in me. In my Father's house there are many dwelling places. If it were not so, would I have told you that I go to prepare a place for you? And if I go and prepare a place for you, I will come again and will take you to myself, so that where I am, you may be also" (John 14:1-3). A room prepared for my loved one, and for me.

### Scripture Meditation: Psalm 91:1-2

You who live in the shelter of the Most High,
who abide in the shadow of the Almighty,
will say to the Lord, "My refuge and my fortress;
my God, in whom I trust."

*My restlessness and my wondering are sometimes satisfying. Sometimes they get the best of me. Regardless of my continual search for the tomorrow beyond, lead me to find my rest in you, O God, my eternal Lord. Amen.*

# Amazing Grace

*In Jesus Christ we come closest to seeing and knowing* the grace of God. Grace, to use one theologian's definition, is "to accept the fact that I'm accepted even though unacceptable." This tries to get at the sheer, total giving of God. It is the undeserved, yet freely given gift of acceptance of us by God in Jesus Christ. This gift reaches in and beyond all we say, do, and go through.

Harvey and Faye said, "As we made our bereavement journey we kept getting the idea that we *had* to go through all the expected feelings and stages. Not only that, we felt we had to go through our mourning well. In other words, it had to be good mourning, not done poorly! We felt constrained to end our journey by affirming life, all put back together. For our mourning to be good, we had to be successful at it!"

But here's where the word of grace came into their lives. They said, "It dawned on us that we didn't have to mourn scientifically or necessarily be successful. God's grace in Jesus Christ meant that even if we weren't able to make our bereavement journey a success, even if we never reached the end, even if we found ourselves in despair, grace embraced us." They were saying that they were accepted in their mourning, even if they were unacceptable and unsuccessful in working it all through.

> Amazing grace! How sweet the sound
> That saved a wretch like me!
> I once was lost, but now am found,
> Was blind, but now I see.
>
> The Lord has promised good to me,
> His word my hope secures;
> He will my shield and portion be
> As long as life endures.

We thank God that he doesn't stand aloof above us, but is involved with his creation. He has redeemed life and death in Christ. Our very bereavement journey is a journey surrounded by and immersed in grace. Thank God!

Let us receive the benediction of grace to our bereavement journey:

*The Lord bless you and keep you. The Lord make his face shine upon you and be gracious unto you, in your going out and in your coming in, in your rising and in your lying down, in your mourning and in your peace, in your labor and in your leisure, in your laughter and in your tears, until you, too, come to stand before him in the day to which there is no sunset and no dawn. In the name of the Father, and of the Son and of the Holy Ghost. Amen.*